The Heart of Acadiana, the Bible, and You

The Heart of Acadiana, the Bible, and You

A 30 DAY
LAFAYETTE DEVOTIONAL

Mark Stipe

PALMETTO
P U B L I S H I N G
Charleston, SC
www.PalmettoPublishing.com

Hardcover ISBN: 979-8-8229-3240-1
Paperback ISBN: 979-8-8229-3241-8
eBook ISBN: 979-8-8229-3242-5

FOREWORD

When Mark first asked me to write the introduction, my first question was: Why me? Certainly, there must be someone who knows him better than I or someone with a deeper understanding of faith and church teaching. And clearly, a person more versed in the history of Lafayette. But the task fell to me, and I told him I would do my best.

I first got to know Mark during our early Dad days when he assumed the coaching job of the SLYSI Bronco's ten-year-old football team. Our sons played together, and to my son Jacob, he was "Coach Mark," a moniker he still uses today. I've never forgotten his knowledge of the game and the love he showed to each player on the team. Like every youth sport, there are those who want to play and others, well, not so much. I remember one instance where one player fumbled the ball near the goal line.

While the face mask on his helmet protected his face from injury, it did little to hide the tears of a little boy who so badly wanted to score a touchdown. Through the sniffles and rapid-fire short breaths, Mark knelt, looked the young man in the eye, and reassured him that it was not his fault. As fate would have it, the young man went on to play high school football and eventually college baseball.

He might not have any remembrances of that day at Neyland Park, but I do, and it warms my heart to this day.

When I read the first manuscript of his book, it all came rushing back. Mark Stipe is still coaching! His book is not about challenging you on matters of religion, nor will it have you searching Wikipedia for answers. To "walk your talk" in today's world is challenging, but Mark has done it concisely.

The book is a trail map of Lafayette's history and the people who helped shape it. He includes scripture passages with the people, places, and events that make Lafayette the special place it is.

At a time when we are often judged by how busy we are, when we wake up every day with our foot on the accelerator, often with minimal direction, Mark's book will serve as a way to slow down, breathe deep, and remember what and WHO in our lives really matter.

I would guess that Mark's inner coaching days are not finished, and when you read this book, you will be glad they are not.

-Marc Mouton

PS: I highly recommend a gold-brick Sunday at Borden's

INTRODUCTION

This is a thirty-day devotional centered on the history, notable residents, land-marks, and culture of Lafayette, Louisiana. My hope is that this book will help you learn a little about Lafayette, and a little about the Bible and Jesus's message.

A habit is just something you do twenty-one days in a row. The ultimate goal of this book is not hidden. The goal is that you read this small book, get in the habit of reading the Bible, and continue to read the Bible and/or a daily devotional long after you have finished this book.

Read one devotional a day. Each devotional is written so that you need only carve out a small amount of time every day to get through it. About twenty years ago, Rick Warren wrote a book entitled *The Purpose Driven Life*. He specifically asked the reader to read one chapter of the book each day "so you will have time to think about the implications for your life."

He went on to say, "One reason most books don't transform us is that we are so eager to read the next chapter, we don't pause to seriously consider what we have just read. We rush to the next truth without reflecting on what we have just learned."

The Bible is our civilization's foundational book. Within its pages is a treasure trove of good stories, great sayings, history, inspirational writing, and the message shared by a presence that came to this earth more than two thousand years ago. It is worth revisiting. Daily.

DAY 1

In the beginning was the Word, and the Word was with God, and the Word was God.

—John 1:1 (New International Version)

Originally established as Vermilionville in the 1820s and incorporated in 1836, Lafayette developed initially as an agricultural community. The introduction of retail and entertainment centers and the discovery of oil in the area in the 1940s helped the area grow. Since the discovery of oil, Lafayette has had a high number of workers in the oil and natural gas industry. With a bond issuance facilitating the construction of a series of roads connecting nearby settlements, the establishment of the University of Louisiana's Lafayette campus, and the continued diversification of the local economy, Lafayette has experienced nearly continuous population growth since its founding.

This once small and rural parish has grown to be the hub city of the third-largest metropolitan area in the state, and it is nicknamed "the Hub City." It is also known as "the Heart of Acadiana" (Hence the title of this devotional).

Things have changed since the founding of Lafayette, and the changes in our world seem to be accelerating. Five-year business plans have yielded to ninety-day plans with meetings along the way to address the changing circumstances. Words, etiquette, and rules are changed for the sake of change, it seems.

The stores, products, institutions, groups, leagues, and brands we grew up with and relied upon are bankrupt or dissolved, purchased, renamed, unfashionable, incorrect, or technologically extinct. Things are changing, and they seem to be changing at an accelerating pace. What is there to rely on?

The Word.

Two thousand years ago, there came a presence on this earth in the form of Jesus Christ. His arrival was foretold in the Old Testament. His teachings and actions are captured in the first books of the New Testament. The way He inspired those around Him is captured in their acts and the letters that make up the remainder of the New Testament.

Those teachings, that wisdom, that approach, that sacrifice—they remain constant. The Bible was a road map two thousand years ago, and it remains a roadmap today. We just have to study it to glean the lessons for living that are in those sixty-six books.

It has sustained us through wars, revolutions, plagues, depressions, migrations, dust bowls, droughts, hurricanes, tornados, and a host of other tests.

We read it today, and the Word will be there for us tomorrow.

DAY 2

All hard work brings a profit, but mere talk leads only to poverty.
—Prov. 14:23 (New International Version)

There have been many, many high school state champions from Lafayette Parish over the years. The question at the beginning of the school year is not whether an athlete or team from Lafayette Parish will win a state championship but how many.

Multiple schools in the parish have won football, basketball, baseball, cross country, golf, swimming, and soccer state championships in the recent past. It would be tough to assemble a list of all the individuals who were either members of a state championship team or won a state championship individually, and if it were done, the list would be long.

That is a testament to the administrations of these schools that put an emphasis on their athletic programs. It is certainly a testament to the coaches who year after year challenge their players to improve, to be good teammates, to maximize their skills and talents, and to apply those habits to other areas of their life.

It starts before high school, obviously. That may be why Lafayette Little League has sent multiple teams to the Little League World Series in the recent past. Parents teach and support their children, and that certainly includes athletics. Strong youth programs help build a good foundation as well. As you will see a bit later, this mindset has generated an impressive list of athletes from Lafayette.

The book of Proverbs contains a lot of, well, proverbs. Pearls of wisdom from centuries ago that can get pushed aside when we don't revisit them regularly. Reading the Bible regularly helps remind us of books in the Bible, like Proverbs.

Perhaps more importantly, reading the Bible regularly helps us to keep things prioritized correctly. Social media campaigns are designed to drown out everything else, or at least shout as loud as everyone else. Timeless values, the proper perspective, the message of Jesus and His teachings—all these can get pushed to the side if we are not careful.

Hard work does pay off, and hard work is not a waste of energy. Sometimes our work toward a state championship produces a state championship. More often, though, hard work produces benefits that we may not realize for a while, and in areas and ways that we never could have envisioned.

Hard work pays off. It is a truism that is rooted in the wisdom of Proverbs, and it is instructive now more than ever.

DAY 3

For in the days of David and Asaph, in ancient times, there were leaders of the singers, songs of praise and hymns of thanksgiving to God.

—Neh. 12:46 (New American Standard Bible)

Speaking to one another with psalms, hymns, and songs from the Spirit. Sing and make music from your heart to the Lord,

—Eph. 5:19 (New International Version)

For a parish of its size, Lafayette Parish may have more Grammy winners per capita than any other area outside of Nashville. A partial list (in alphabetical order):

The Band Courtbouillon

BeauSoleil

Buckwheat Zydeco

Chubby Carrier and the Bayou Swamp Band

Clifton Chenier

Lauren Daigle

Lost Bayou Ramblers

Rockin' Sidney

Terrance Simien and the Zydeco Experience

Lafayette hosts the Festival International de Louisiane in downtown Lafayette annually. It rivals Jazz Fest in New Orleans, but there really is no rivalry. The two groups coordinate bookings to make it more attractive for faraway musical groups to travel to and perform at both events.

The Lafayette High band is a powerhouse that is recognized across the state and nation for its excellence. The Lafayette High band (along with the Acadiana High band) actually performed at President Jimmy Carter's inauguration. There is a Latin music festival in town, and a zydeco festival and an accordion festival are a short drive away from Lafayette. If you like to line dance, you can do it to "Cupid Shuffle" (he is from Lafayette too).

The Cajundome is a frequent stop for touring concert performers. The Heymann Performing Arts Center is a smaller venue that hosts touring groups and artists, and the Acadiana Center for the Arts is an intimate venue that hosts performers as well.

The point being that for those of us who love live music, or dancing, or both, there are plenty of opportunities available. We can sing along or just enjoy the talent of the professionals.

Singing is a part of celebrating Jesus's message and sacrifice. Most all denominations and services incorporate two or three songs of praise into each service. Some hymnals even have tips for singing to help parishioners. Take that to mean everyone should participate.

There is something in the human heart that expresses through music the joy and sorrow that cannot be expressed otherwise.

For those of us that are less than confident about our musical talents, fear not. There is no record of any attendee being thrown out of a service or mass for bad singing, at least not in Lafayette Parish. The congregations seem to be pretty forgiving groups. Jesus brought good news, and we can feel free to sing about it (even if we are off key).

DAY 4

Jesus entered the temple courts and drove out all who were buying and selling there. He overturned the tables of the money changers and the benches of those selling doves. "It is written," he said to them, "'My house will be called a house of prayer,' but you are making it 'a den of robbers.'" The blind and the lame came to him at the temple, and he healed them.

—Matt. 21:12–14 (New International Version)

There are a number of beautiful places to worship in Lafayette. In the downtown area alone, there are the Cathedral of St. John, First Baptist, First Methodist, Ascension Episcopal, and Temple Shalom. Recently, St. Pius and Our Savior's Church have constructed impressive sanctuaries. One hesitates to list those, because for every one that is mentioned there are just as many others that are just as beautiful.

Beautiful sanctuaries can be found all across the parish, each with its own unique qualities, style, and attention to detail. And each one with parishioners that funded the construction and continue funding the maintenance of those sanctuaries to preserve their beauty.

Jesus made it clear that the temples were for worship and good works. He got angry when a temple was used for something else. Two separate points here.

First, Jesus got angry. Elsewhere in the Bible, the shortest verse declares "Jesus wept." There was good reason for Him to do so on both occasions. Every now and again, there is good reason for us to get angry as well. Anger should be warranted, and it probably shouldn't become a daily occurrence. There is also good reason to weep every now and again as we work through the valleys of life. Anger, sorrow, joy; these are human emotions. If we are trying to practice Christianity, we shouldn't let someone put us on the defensive and mock our Christianity because we fall short of the glory of God. We also shouldn't let someone rob us of a joyous moment because being overjoyed is not "Christian." We were made in God's image; emotion is something we both have.

Second, God's house is made for worship. We should use it for its intended purpose. The efforts and resources spent by the parishioners at every house of worship in the parish are admirable, and we should respect those efforts.

Block off some time and take a tour of the houses of worship in Lafayette. To see them all, you will need to block off a lot. The number of beautiful structures maintained in Lafayette speaks well for the parish as a whole. It means—among other things—that stewardship of these structures is a priority for each of the congregations.

Better yet, we should enjoy a service at our chosen house of worship. Weekly. There is certainly no shortage of options.

DAY 5

"We have here only five loaves of bread and two fish," they answered.
—Matt. 14:17 (New International Version)

Jesus replied, "You give them something to eat." They answered, "We have only five loaves of bread and two fish—unless we go and buy food for all this crowd." (About five thousand men were there.)
—Luke 9:13 (New International Version)

Oh, the restaurants. So, so many so worthy of mention. Lafayette is an internationally recognized culinary center.

Perhaps it is because the importance of family meals around the dinner table spills over to retail establishments. Perhaps it is because of the importance of client entertainment in the oil industry, which historically made dining out so important. Perhaps it is because good cooking just lends itself to cooks that want to open restaurants. Perhaps it is because of the close proximity to seafood, game, crawfish, rice, peppers, and sugar; good food is made easier when so many fresh ingredients are nearby.

Whatever the reason, there are an incredible number of restaurants in Lafayette. Cajun, Creole, Mexican, Tex-Mex, Japanese, Italian, Mediterranean, and BBQ are here. Fine dining, bistros, casual spots, and even sports bars with high-quality food are all available.

EatLafayette.com is a website devoted to locally owned restaurants in the area. There are ninety restaurants and eateries listed as of this writing. You can view the list alphabetically, group the restaurants geographically, and see the list broken down into categories. It is an impressive list of establishments, but keep in mind not all the restaurants in Lafayette are locally owned. That is not an exhaustive list of the restaurants in Lafayette.

There is something about sharing a meal that brings fellowship along with it. In a later section of this devotional, we will talk about how to jump-start the discussion at the dinner table if it is necessary. However, one way that is always appropriate is to thank the cook.

This story of fishes and loaves is a miracle. It also solved a pressing problem. Five thousand men (together with women and children) who are hungry can turn into an unruly crowd in a hurry.

Jesus solved that problem two thousand years ago. He also showed us how to solve problems that confront us today. Through teachings, parables, actions, responses to questions, and sacrifice, Jesus left us a road map for confronting life's challenges. God does care about our material and physical needs, and He will provide for us.

His message through parables, teachings, actions, and His ultimate sacrifice and resurrection set out the guidelines and support for dealing with the problems we confront today. We just need to read His message to us.

DAY 6

They brought the donkey and the colt and placed their cloaks on them
for Jesus to sit on. A very large crowd spread their cloaks on the road,
while others cut branches from the trees and spread them on the road.
The crowds that went ahead of him and those that followed shouted...

—Matt. 21:7–9 (New International Version)

While Lafayette has embraced the tradition of celebrating Mardi Gras annually since 1897, planning for an annual Lafayette Mardi Gras celebration started in 1933, when the Greater Southwest Louisiana Mardi Gras Association was formed. It was deemed important by business leaders to have a citywide celebration that all residents could enjoy. The vision of a few business leaders who had the wherewithal to step up ensured that Mardi Gras would continue during hard times.

Maurice Heymann was the leader among the small group of organizers who formed the Greater Southwest Louisiana Mardi Gras Association with the goal of assuming the responsibility of putting on Mardi Gras for Lafayette. In fact, many credit Maurice Heymann as being the "father of Lafayette's Mardi Gras" because he underwrote the group's activities many times until the organization was on sound financial footing. Lafayette Mardi Gras was suspended from 1944 to 1946 due to World War II and in 2021 due to the COVID-19 pandemic, but other than those two hiatuses, it has run continually since the Greater Southwest Mardi Gras Association has coordinated the event.

Lafayette has over the years developed a family-friendly Mardi Gras celebration. There are four nights of parades that roll through the city before Fat Tuesday, and of course a number of parades that roll on Fat Tuesday.

Most parades start at Pontiac Point, east of the Evangeline Thruway, wind through downtown, then roll down Johnston Street before ending at Cajun Field. It is about a five-mile route, and on Fat Tuesday the route is lined with people, sometimes twenty deep, catching the throws from the floats. In addition to the floats, high school marching bands, dance teams, a steel drum band, motorcycles, classic cars, elected officials, and the Boy Scouts are part of the parades as well. There are a carnival and performances nightly at Cajun Field in the weeks leading up to Fat Tuesday, and, of course, this is all presided over by a "king" and "queen." The other municipalities in Lafayette Parish also have parades that roll through their towns during the Mardi Gras season.

Jesus rode into Jerusalem with cheering crowds all along His route. The celebration turned somber quickly; Palm Sunday turns to Good Friday. The celebration did not last. Mardi Gras crowds don't either. They cheer for the float riders as they pass, but then they move on to the next float coming down the road. Once the parades end, the crowds move on, the street sweepers move in, and the cleanup begins.

After Mardi Gras, Lent begins. For Jesus, events in a few days would bring on horrific suffering and death, which He endured for us.

So many in the world crave "likes" and followers. Social media has created a different value system. Our social media presence matters; it is everything in the world to some. However, in the world of social media, impressive postings, Instagram stories, and tweets are drowned out by the social media postings of the next day. Social media campaigns are designed to overlay yesterday's social media postings. It seems so fleeting. Because it is.

Worldly adulation is a fleeting thing, but Jesus did not come for worldly adulation. He came to deliver a new message, to live out that message, and through His suffering, death, and resurrection to show how much He wants us to embrace that message.

DAY 7

This is the genealogy of Jesus the Messiah the son of David, the son of Abraham...

—Matt. 1:1 (New International Version)

The beginning of the good news about Jesus the Messiah, the Son of God...

—Mark 1:1 (New International Version)

Many have undertaken to draw up an account of the things that have been fulfilled among us...

—Luke 1:1 (New International Version)

In the beginning was the Word, and the Word was with God, and the Word was God.

—John 1:1 (New International Version)

Attakapas Indians, whose population was concentrated along the Vermilion River, were the primary residents of the Lafayette area before the French colonization. After the Louisiana Purchase, American settlers began moving into the area and intermarrying among the French, enslaved Africans, and free people of color. Since 1860, Lafayette has grown from 498 to 121,374 residents as of the 2020 US census.

If you look at the census data for Lafayette, the composition of Lafayette's population looks like this:

Racial and ethnic composition	2020	2010	2000
Non-Hispanic/Latino white	56.95%	63.78%	68.50%
African Americans	30.5%	31.11%	28.25%
Hispanic or Latino (of any race)	6.2%	3.76%	1.88%
Asian Americans	2.58%	1.81%	1.42%
Pacific Islander	0.03%	n/a	n/a
Two or more races	3.45%	1.68%	0.98%

It appears from the table above that Lafayette is something of a melting pot. Indeed it is. A variety of cultures, religious denominations, and ethnic groups are present and accounted for in Lafayette. As a result, a variety of perspectives on matters exists in Lafayette.

There are four Gospels in the New Testament, written by four disciples. Four disciples, four completely different ways to start the story of Jesus's time on this earth.

Which was right? The answer is all of them. Each was divinely inspired.

However, every human being will have a different perspective on things. No two people will view an event, a person, or an incident exactly the same way. All humans view the world through the lens of the time they grew up, where they grew up, events that happened while they were growing up, the perception of those in the community, and so many other factors.

It is interesting to study the roster of the disciples. It was a diverse group. The only commonality was Jesus.

John's Gospel was written by a beloved disciple and focuses on who Jesus is. Matthew's Gospel was written by a tax collector and focuses on what Jesus said. Luke was a doctor, and his Gospel focuses on how Jesus felt. Mark's Gospel focuses on what Jesus did.

There is a right and a wrong. The Bible sets out the guidelines for all of us. However, it is also helpful to understand the perspective of the people with whom we are interacting. This is not to say we need to walk in their shoes, but it does help to know where the shoes have been.

Episcopal Church of the Ascension

DAY 8

Similarly, anyone who competes as an athlete does not receive the victor's crown except by competing according to the rules.

—2 Tim. 2:5 (New International Version)

The list of professional athletes from Lafayette Parish is deep and impressive. A partial list (in alphabetical order):

Paul Bako

David Benoit

Hollis Conway

Daniel Cormier

Jake Delhomme

Kent Desormeaux

Armand "Mondo" Duplantis

Kevin Faulk

Jerry Fontenot

Ron Guidry

Mikie Mahtook

Gil Meche

Justin Poirier

Chanda Rubin

And so many more…

All of them possess exceptional skills or talents that—along with hard work—allowed them to excel in their chosen sports. The importance of discipline is the overarching theme of 2 Timothy's second chapter.

"I wish God had given me talent so I could be as good as they are," we say to ourselves. Ah, but He did.

God placed us on this earth for a reason, with special and unique talents and gifts. Our skills and talents are a gift from God; what we do with them is our gift to Him.

Another aspect of our presence on this earth must be emphasized. To put it bluntly, what we individually do matters. Most of us likely don't have a Super Bowl ring, a championship belt, or a world record. We ask ourselves, "What does it matter what I do?"

Well, it does. Our actions influence our family, our friends, and others around us. We never know when a kind gesture, a helping hand, or an encouraging note can change the direction of someone's life.

Lou Holtz was a college football coach for many years and at many schools. He used to say that there are about a hundred fifty plays in a football game, and about ten will determine the outcome. The problem is you really don't know which ten it is until the game is over. That is part of our challenge: to live like a champion at all times because we never know when our actions will be an inflection point for another person.

What we do matters. What we do and how we do it—that is part of our gift to God.

Confessing their sins, they were baptized by him in the Jordan River.

—Matt. 3:6 (New International Version)

The Vermilion River runs through the heart of Lafayette. Johnston Street and Kaliste Saloom Road essentially run parallel to each other for most of their length, and the Vermilion River winds between the two, through the city and all the way to the Vermilion Parish line.

It is one of the more inaccessible rivers that runs through a major US city. You can see it and access it at a handful of points around the Evangeline Thruway, at Rotary Point, at Pinhook Road, at Camellia Boulevard, and in Milton.

If you travel down the river by boat, you will see what seems like an endless number of beautiful homes on both sides of the river. Residential housing occupies, by and large, the area between the river and the two roads running along each side of the river.

In some areas of the country, "water rights" means a fight over who gets the water that is available. That is not the issue in Lafayette; instead, drainage of the abundant water is.

Water plays a prominent role in the New Testament. Baptism in the Jordan River, turning water into wine, Jesus walking across water, the disciples fishing in the sea—there are so many ways water played a role in Jesus's teachings.

We need water. It can bring a fresh start by washing away a mistake or a problem. It can bring revitalization in the form of rain. Like so much of what we have, it can be destructive if we do not properly manage it. It is almost like we need a guidebook to help us manage our use of water...

The Bible, too, can bring us a fresh start by providing guidance on a mistake or a problem. The Bible can bring us revitalization through the psalms or the reading of proverbs and inspirational stories. What is destructive is to ignore a book that is foundational to our civilization. The guidebook is there; we just need to read it.

But a poor widow came and put in two very small copper coins, worth only a few cents.

Calling his disciples to him, Jesus said, "Truly I tell you, this poor widow has put more into the treasury than all the others. They all gave out of their wealth; but she, out of her poverty, put in everything—all she had to live on."

—Mark 12:42–44 (New International Version)

Moncus Park is a hundred-acre park in the center of Lafayette.

In 1920, when the University of Louisiana at Lafayette (UL Lafayette) purchased it for agricultural research, it was beyond the city limits. Lafayette continued to grow around it. It housed cows, then horses, earning the nickname "the Horse Farm."

In 2005, UL Lafayette announced plans to allow for commercial development at the farm. Citizens launched a "Save the Horse Farm" campaign to instead preserve the property as a central park for everyone in the community. In 2012, UL Lafayette sold the land to the City of Lafayette under the leadership of Mayor-President Joey Durel, who also championed this idea of a new park. With the support of thousands of advocates, the property, at last, had been "saved."

In May 2016, Moncus Park was announced as the new name of the park in appreciation for the very generous gift from the late Jim Moncus, a philanthropist in the Lafayette community.

It is rightfully named after Jim Moncus. His transformational gift(s) jump-started plans and construction at the park. However, he was not alone in giving to support the project. Many, many groups and individuals contributed and continue to contribute to the project.

The widow's contribution was, comparatively speaking, small. But it was significant for her. "Significant" can be a relative term. What's more, it is easy to convince ourselves that since our gift is not significant, there is no need to make the effort; it is easy to persuade ourselves that "no one will notice it" or "no one will miss my little contribution" or "the little bit I could contribute won't make a difference."

But each of our contributions is important. Our interactions influence others, one way or the other. Our contribution challenges those around us to give, and our avoidance of a contribution discourages those around us from contributing. That goes for whether we lend a hand to a neighbor needing a little more muscle for a home improvement project, stop to help someone who looks like a lost tourist, or simply pick up a piece of trash that someone threw on the ground. Those are contributions too. Do not minimize the effects of those little contributions. They do influence those around us to do the same.

What do Jim Moncus and the widow have in common? They both gave what they had. When a lot of people make what is for them a significant contribution, good things often happen. Good things for the project, and good things for the contributors too.

DAY 11

Similarly, encourage the young men to be self-controlled. In everything set them an example by doing what is good. In your teaching show integrity, seriousness and soundness of speech that cannot be condemned, so that those who oppose you may be ashamed because they have nothing bad to say about us.

—Titus 2:6–10 (New International Version)

36

Tony Robichaux was the head coach of the Ragin' Cajun baseball team from 1995 until his death in 2019. He won 910 games at UL Lafayette and 1173 college games overall. He took the Ragin' Cajuns to eleven NCAA tournament appearances, four Super Regional appearances in the NCAA tournament, and the NCAA College World Series. A great baseball coach.

As good a coach as he was, he was a better teacher. He taught his players to be hardworking, disciplined, polite, focused, and good representatives of the university and the baseball program. He viewed the game of baseball as a vehicle to teach young men to be good citizens, good employees, good husbands, and good parents.

During one baseball season, he travelled over to Lafayette Little League to talk to the parents about the way to approach teaching baseball to kids and how to handle travel ball. What major college baseball coach in the middle of the season carves out time to speak to Little League parents? He did.

If you drive around town, you will see the number 36 on the back windshields of cars and trucks. That was the number he wore as a coach, and that number 36 on the windshields is in honor of him.

When he passed away, the visitation was moved to the convention center to accommodate all those coming to pay their respects.

That immense respect and appreciation did not get created in a day. The baseball program he built was not constructed overnight. It was built decision by decision, day by day, month by month, and season after season.

Strive each time to be an example, to do what is right, to do what is needed even if what is needed requires hard work.

In the words of Paul, be an example. In everything and every day. Day after day, month after month, year after year. The ability to be persistent, to work hard, to be an example—those are talents. Give those back to God.

DAY 12

Hearing that Jesus had silenced the Sadducees, the Pharisees got together. One of them, an expert in the law, tested him with this question: "Teacher, which is the greatest commandment in the Law?"

Jesus replied: "Love the Lord your God with all your heart and with all your soul and with all your mind." This is the first and greatest commandment. And the second is like it: 'Love your neighbor as yourself.' All the Law and the Prophets hang on these two commandments."

—Matt. 22:34–40 (New International Version)

And when the days of the Pentecost were accomplished, they were all together in one place:

And suddenly there came a sound from heaven, as of a mighty wind coming, and it filled the whole house where they were sitting. And there appeared to them parted tongues as it were of fire, and it sat upon every one of them. And they were all filled with the Holy Ghost, and they began to speak with diverse tongues, according as the Holy Ghost gave them to speak.

—Acts 2:1–4 (Douay-Rheims Bible)

The first recorded Red Mass was celebrated in the Cathedral of Paris in 1245. In certain localities of France, the Red Mass was celebrated in honor of Saint Ives, the Patron Saint of Lawyers. From there, it spread to most European countries. The tradition began in England around 1310, during the reign of Edward II. It was attended at the opening of each term of Court by all members of the Bench and Bar.

The Red Mass is so called from the red vestments traditionally worn in symbolism of the tongues of fire (the Holy Spirit) that descended on the Apostles at Pentecost (the second scripture above). Its name also exemplifies the scarlet robes worn by royal judges who attended the Mass centuries ago.

Lafayette's civil courts used to take the summer off. In the fall there was a court opening ceremony—new members of the Bar were recognized, as well as attorneys who had passed away since the last court opening. There was also a Red Mass at the Cathedral of St. John that was attended by the judiciary and members of the Bar.

The Cathedral of St. John the Evangelist

Lafayette courts now operate year round. The court opening in Lafayette cannot now be tracked to a specific "opening day," but the ceremony is still held. Perhaps most importantly and thankfully, Red Mass at the Cathedral of St. John continues on, and the Bishop of the Catholic Diocese of Lafayette has been in attendance for at least the last thirty years.

Often, we get focused on the rules. If we follow the rules, we will be all right. Rules are important, but compliance with rules seems to flow naturally when our hearts are right.

The Pharisees had become too enmeshed in the rules. Memorizing the rules, teaching the rules, administering the rules, enforcing the rules, and using the rules against people. Sometimes when the focus is just on the rules, the rationale behind a rule gets subverted. The reason for the rule begins to get lost.

Again, rules are important, but compliance with the rules seems to flow naturally when our hearts are right. The message of Jesus and his disciples is to get our hearts right and love our neighbors. Those are the two overarching commandments. They are not necessarily easy, but they are simple.

DAY 13

Paul, a prisoner of Christ Jesus, and Timothy our brother,

To Philemon our dear friend and fellow worker—also to Apphia our sister and Archippus our fellow soldier—and to the church that meets in your home:

Grace and peace to you from God our Father and the Lord Jesus Christ.

I always thank my God as I remember you in my prayers, because I hear about your love for all his holy people and your faith in the Lord Jesus. I pray that your partnership with us in the faith may be effective in deepening your understanding of every good thing we share for the sake of Christ. Your love has given me great joy and encouragement, because you, brother, have refreshed the hearts of the Lord's people.

Therefore, although in Christ I could be bold and order you to do what you ought to do, yet I prefer to appeal to you on the basis of love. It is as none other than Paul—an old man and now also a prisoner of Christ Jesus—that I appeal to you for my son Onesimus, who became my son while I was in chains. Formerly he was useless to you, but now he has become useful both to you and to me.

I am sending him—who is my very heart—back to you. I would have liked to keep him with me so that he could take your place in help-ing me while I am in chains for the gospel. But I did not want to do anything without your consent, so that any favor you do would not seem forced but would be voluntary. Perhaps the reason he was separated from you for a little while was that you might have him back forever—no longer as a slave, but better than a slave, as a dear brother. He is very dear to me but even dearer to you, both as a fellow man and as a brother in the Lord.

So if you consider me a partner, welcome him as you would welcome me. If he has done you any wrong or owes you anything, charge it to me. I, Paul, am writing this with my own hand. I will pay it back—not to mention that you owe me your very self. I do wish, brother, that I may have some benefit from you in the Lord; refresh my heart in Christ. Confident of your obedience, I write to you, knowing that you will do even more than I ask.

And one thing more: Prepare a guest room for me, because I hope to be restored to you in answer to your prayers.

Epaphras, my fellow prisoner in Christ Jesus, sends you greetings. And so do Mark, Aristarchus, Demas and Luke, my fellow workers.

The grace of the Lord Jesus Christ be with your spirit.

—Phil. 1 (New International Version)

Freetown-Port Rico is a Lafayette neighborhood that once was a safe haven for freed slaves and is listed on the National Register of Historic Places. The Freetown-Port Rico neighborhood is bounded by East University Avenue, Lee Avenue, Garfield Street, Taft Street, Lucille Avenue, Jefferson Street, and Coolidge Street.

Sugar cane was once grown on the neighborhood's soil, which was once the back part of Alexander Mouton's Île Copal Plantation. Mouton was a nineteenth-century Louisiana governor and US senator.

The neighborhood formed during the Civil War period and was a place where newly freed slaves and the original free men of color could create a community.

Philemon is one of the shorter books of the Bible. The focus of this book was largely centered on the issue of slavery. Those opposed to the abolition of slavery often cited it as biblical support for their position.

There are twenty-five verses in the whole book. It is a letter, like a majority of the books of the New Testament. There is a lot packed into those twenty-five verses to be studied, however: Paul paying the debt of a slave, the free gift of freedom from slavery, the response of Onesimus (which was to spend the rest of his life spreading the message).

A different point presents itself regarding this book of the Bible, however. As a fun exercise, try typing the letter on your laptop, computer, or iPhone. While it may take a while, consider that Paul wrote this without any of those. No autocorrect, no backspace, no Wite-Out. Just a handwritten letter on whatever paper was available. (Somewhat ironically, technological advances have made a handwritten note even more powerful because it is so rare.)

The last point is to stress the importance of setting aside time each day to read the Bible. We have a lot of things and tasks to deal with every day. They crowd out the time and energy we have for each day. However, we just read an entire book of the Bible. We just carved out time to read an entire book of the Bible. We did it today, and we can do it tomorrow.

The elder,

To my dear friend Gaius, whom I love in the truth.

Dear friend, I pray that you may enjoy good health and that all may go well with you, even as your soul is getting along well. It gave me great joy when some believers came and testified about your faithfulness to the truth, telling how you continue to walk in it. I have no greater joy than to hear that my children are walking in the truth.

Dear friend, you are faithful in what you are doing for the brothers and sisters, even though they are strangers to you. They have told the church about your love. Please send them on their way in a manner that honors God. It was for the sake of the Name that they went out, receiving no help from the pagans. We ought therefore to show hospitality to such people so that we may work together for the truth.

I wrote to the church, but Diotrephes, who loves to be first, will not welcome us. So when I come, I will call attention to what he is doing, spreading malicious nonsense about us. Not satisfied with that, he even refuses to welcome other believers. He also stops those who want to do so and puts them out of the church.

Dear friend, do not imitate what is evil but what is good. Anyone who does what is good is from God. Anyone who does what is evil has not seen God. Demetrius is well spoken of by everyone—and even by the truth itself. We also speak well of him, and you know that our testimony is true.

I have much to write you, but I do not want to do so with pen and ink. I hope to see you soon, and we will talk face to face.

Peace to you. The friends here send their greetings. Greet the friends there by name.

—3 John 1 (English Standard Version)

There are a number of notable writers that have lived in Lafayette and the surrounding area in the recent past. Gus Weill was a Lafayette native. Carl Brasseaux documented Cajun history in his writings. Earnest Gaines was on the faculty at UL Lafayette. John Ed Bradley lived in Opelousas but used to play basketball in the Lafayette Parks & Rec leagues. Bob Hamm had a radio show on Saturday mornings at one time in addition to writing his books on the area. While James Lee Burke's home is in New Iberia, don't be surprised if you look across the room at a Lafayette restaurant and see him breaking bread with friends and relatives. All of them are noted authors with national recognition.

Some are without national recognition too (so far). Dr. Bryan Sibley is a local pediatrician who wrote a book recently about his challenges in discerning the right priorities. Jill Duhon recently completed a children's book. Steve Rabalais wrote a biography about General Fox Conner. There are of course multiple Grammy-winning songwriters from Lafayette.

More than half the books of the New Testament are letters. A person wanted to share a message with another person, group, or congregation. He composed his thoughts, reduced those thoughts to writing, and transmitted them to the recipient.

That effort generated a powerful message that still provides benefit to the people reading it two thousand years later. That is the case even though we were not the intended recipient of the letter. In the scripture above, John challenges his friend to imitate what is good. Still good advice for our friends today.

Letters still send a powerful message. As mentioned yesterday, technology has had the effect of making a handwritten message even more powerful. As with those letters in the New Testament, our effort in composing and sending a letter resonates with the recipient. Now more than ever.

(By the way, congratulate yourself. You just read another book of the Bible today.)

DAY 15

In the land of Uz there lived a man whose name was Job...he owned seven thousand sheep, three thousand camels, five hundred yoke of oxen and five hundred donkeys, and had a large number of servants. He was the greatest man among all the people of the East.

—Job 1:1–3 (New International Version)

Jim Moncus travelled to Lafayette because he heard there were jobs in the area, and he needed a job badly. He found one in the oil industry and immediately went offshore because it offered a bed to sleep in at night and food to eat (neither of which he had). He went on to build several successful businesses and was a noted philanthropist. Pretty good considering he started from scratch.

Matt Stuller started selling jewelry out of the trunk of his car. He built the business into the largest wholesale supplier of jewelry in the nation and one of the largest private companies in the area. There are other notable entrepreneurs referenced in other devotional pages.

There are dozens of Horatio Alger–like stories about Lafayette citizens. What's more, there are hundreds of stories of family-owned companies where the second generation stood on the shoulders of the first generation. The second generation took the business to new and unprecedented heights, building a life for its members and employment for hundreds of people.

Job was a wealthy man. Seven thousand sheep is a lot now—imagine what it represented before the time of Jesus. However, the book of Job is about Job's trials and tribulations.

We see people who are successful, and we think they have it easy—they must not have a thing to worry about. Some people want to take away what successful people have, arguing they don't deserve to live "with that much."

However, most of the time, people really don't know how hard others worked to achieve success or how talented they really are. They are successful. However, we don't work with them on a day-to-day basis, and we aren't there to see how someone who is successful has worked through the rough patches of life. People just see (and fixate on) the end result. History shows us that success is, generally speaking, very much earned.

First United Methodist Church

More importantly, successful people have the same challenges as every other person. We all worry about our kids; we fight with our spouses; some of us get divorced. We all get sick; our kids and family members get sick. We all have to work through tragic accidents and wrestle with bad habits.

The book of Job is a reminder that the valleys of life are universal. We all have challenges. The good news is God is with us through all of them. Jesus came, in part, to teach us and show us how to deal with those challenges. If we put God in charge, we can and will work through all those challenges.

DAY 16

One day Jesus said to his disciples, "Let us go over to the other side of the lake." So they got into a boat and set out.

—Luke 8:22 (New International Version)

When Jesus heard what had happened, he withdrew by boat privately to a solitary place.

—Matt. 14:13 (New International Version)

Again Jesus began to teach by the lake. The crowd that gathered around him was so large that he got into a boat and sat in it out on the lake, while all the people were along the shore at the water's edge.

—Mark 4:1 (New International Version)

If you want to get in a boat on the water, Lafayette gives you lots of options.

The Atchafalaya Swamp is twenty minutes to the east. Vermilion Bay is a forty-minute drive south southeast. Rockefeller Refuge is a ninety-minute drive southwest. Three Mile Lake is forty minutes north, in St. Landry Parish.

A river runs through Lafayette.

Bodies of water figure prominently during many important times of Jesus's ministry. Whether it was a way to speak to a crowd, a way to calm the fears of his disciples, or just to have solitude for discernment, Jesus made use of a boat.

Boats allow us to glide across the water, moving from point A to point B quickly and efficiently. Boats allow us to go to a secluded fishing spot in the basin, pull a skier across the lake, head along the coast to catch speckled trout, or just cruise in the party barge at sunset.

In South Louisiana, water and boats can evoke memories of a great time on the water. They can also evoke memories of a hurricane, which involves lots of unwanted water. The Cajun Navy, which started as an assembly of volunteers piloting flat-bottomed boats, has come to the rescue repeatedly in recent years in South Louisiana after disasters to help with the recovery. It has grown in size and structure and now has a reach outside Louisiana in assisting disaster recovery efforts.

Boats lift us above the water level during recreation in the basin or in the aftermath of a disaster. Jesus's message and miracles lifted up countless followers then and still do today.

The verses following Luke 8:22 are instructive. In sum, Jesus fell asleep as they crossed the lake, and a squall came down and endangered everyone on the boat. The disciples woke Jesus, who promptly got up, calmed the waters, and asked the disciples "Where is your faith?"

We will face stormy winds and raging waters. It is in those moments that we should locate our faith, not run from it.

DAY 17

And he sent them out to proclaim the kingdom of God and to heal the sick.

—Luke 9:2 (New International Version)

They drove out many demons and anointed many sick people with oil and healed them.

—Mark 6.13 (New International Version)

Lafayette is blessed with multiple hospital systems that have a presence in the area, a number of specialty hospitals and surgical centers, and several clinics that can provide urgent or emergency care.

Our Lady of Lourdes is the longest continually owned and operated hospital in Lafayette, having been built in 1949. Bishop Jules Benjamin Jeanmard, the first bishop of the Lafayette Diocese, was instrumental in encouraging the construction of the hospital in Lafayette. Sister Agnes Fitzsimons served as president of Our Lady of Lourdes from 1966 to 1985.

The main campus for Our Lady of Lourdes moved to its current location in 2012. Women's & Children's Hospital, Heart Hospital, and Park Place Surgical Hospital are also part of that system.

Lafayette General Medical Center was started as a locally owned hospital in 1911, owned by a nonprofit corporation whose board was composed of Lafayette citizens. It has been operating continuously since its founding, but it did move to its current location in 1965. In 2021 ownership was transferred to the Ochsner Health System. The main campus is in the Oil Center, and the hospitals on Ambassador Caffery Parkway and Congress Street are also part of that system.

University Medical Center is the charity hospital in Lafayette. The management of that hospital was recently taken over by Lafayette General Medical Center.

There are a dozen or so walk-in clinics, freestanding emergency rooms, and surgery centers across Lafayette Parish. It has become a health-care hub for the region.

Jesus restores people, and spiritually He gives us new life. Healing the sick was part of what Jesus did and part of what He charged His disciples to do. It was a component of His ministry, and that component of His ministry continues today through the works of the health-care professionals across the parish.

In an earlier devotional, the Red Mass was explained. Health-care professionals also have a White Coat Mass annually that celebrates the efforts, challenges, and contributions of the health-care professionals in Lafayette Parish.

Jesus spent a good deal of time healing those that were afflicted with a variety of maladies. As you read the Gospels, you find a dozen or so specific instances of healing an afflicted person. He healed many more, of course. In Matthew 9, it is explained that He went through towns and villages "healing **every** disease and sickness." (Emphasis added.) Restoring people was a key component of His ministry. He even got criticism from the Pharisees for healing on the Sabbath.

Faith and healing go together. "There are no atheists in foxholes," goes the saying. There aren't many in preop either.

DAY 18

For everything there is a season, and a time for every matter under
heaven:
a time to be born, and a time to die;
a time to plant, and a time to pluck up what is planted;
a time to kill, and a time to heal;
a time to break down, and a time to build up;
a time to weep, and a time to laugh;
a time to mourn, and a time to dance;
a time to cast away stones, and a time to gather stones together;
a time to embrace, and a time to refrain from embracing;
a time to seek, and a time to lose;
a time to keep, and a time to cast away;
a time to tear, and a time to sew;
a time to keep silence, and a time to speak;
a time to love, and a time to hate;
a time for war, and a time for peace.

—Eccles. 3:1–8 (English Standard Version)

Various weather sources describe Lafayette's weather as a humid subtropical climate typical of the southern United States, with moderate temperatures and abundant precipitation. Summers can be very hot and humid, with temperatures often reaching the upper nineties, while winters are mild but occasionally cold, with lows sometimes dropping into the midtwenties. Rainfall is plentiful throughout the year, averaging around forty-eight inches annually. Thunderstorms are frequent during spring and summer months, bringing frequent lightning strikes and brief downpours.

On average, there are 217 sunny days per year in Lafayette. The US average is 205 sunny days.

Lafayette gets some kind of precipitation, on average, 108 days per year. The summer high is in July, when the average high temperature is ninety-one degrees. The winter low is in January, when the average temperature is forty-two degrees.

While there are seasonal norms, if you live in Lafayette long enough, you will experience a full range of weather. Ask any resident who has lived in Lafayette for more than thirty years, and that person can tell you about a time when it snowed, when it froze, when the Vermilion River flooded because it rained nonstop, when there was a drought because there was no rain, or when a hurricane went through the area.

Life is like that too. As the scripture suggests, we will experience a range of seasons during our time on this earth. Some will be joyous; some will be painful. God is with us through both the peaks and valleys of life, but He never said there wouldn't be valleys.

We will have valleys to walk through in life. In those times we will be presented with a choice. We can work to overcome those challenges or let those challenges consume our spirit. Broadly stated, two voices in society will be speaking to us.

One is the voice of perseverance. The exhortations of Norman Vincent Peale, John Wooden, and their successors—inspired by the Bible—will comfort you and give you strength to work through these challenges.

Other voices will speak to you with a different message. They suggest we find and assess blame for the challenge we are confronting, dwell on the emotion caused by the challenge, and spend energy focusing on the magnitude of the challenge. Unfortunately, we will likely hear these voices much more often in today's society. A lot of times there is a financial motivation for those voices, and generally speaking, they do not have your best interests at heart.

Jesus does.

His message will guide you through the challenge. His example(s) in dealing with challenges will guide you through the storm.

One family dinner conversation starter is to go around the table and ask for each family member at the table to describe the "peak and the pit" of that particular day.

There are almost always a peak and a pit every day. There certainly will be peaks and pits during the course of our lives. The good news is that God is with us through both.

DAY 19

In reply Jesus said: "A man was going down from Jerusalem to Jericho,
when he was attacked by robbers. They stripped him of his clothes, beat
him and went away, leaving him half dead. A priest happened to be
going down the same road, and when he saw the man, he passed by on
the other side. So too, a Levite, when he came to the place and saw him,
passed by on the other side. But a Samaritan, as he traveled, came where
the man was; and when he saw him, he took pity on him. He went to him
and bandaged his wounds, pouring on oil and wine. Then he put the man
on his own donkey, brought him to an inn and took care of him.

—Luke 10:30–34 (New International Version)

Johnston Street was for quite some time the main drag for Lafayette. Years ago if you were looking for someplace and were told "it's right off Johnston," that didn't help much, because pretty much the whole town was off Johnston Street.

Other traffic arteries have been built or improved. However, Johnston Street is still a main artery and the most direct way to get to Abbeville.

In Lafayette it is primarily a five-lane road with no median, just an unending turning lane. Unfortunately, many people use that turning lane as an on-ramp and accelerate as they merge into the left lane.

It really doesn't help to speed down Johnston Street. Almost invariably the car that speeds by you ends up next to you at the next traffic light. The best way to navigate Johnston Street is to leave ten minutes earlier than you planned and relax while en route.

The parable of the Good Samaritan on the surface seems straight-forward and simple. If you encounter someone that needs help, stop and help the person. As you study things more, however, you learn that Samaritans were hated, and the initial reaction to be expected was for the Samaritan to step over the man and keep on going. The reaction of the Good Samaritan is totally unexpected absurd kindness.

There are simple answers. They are not always easy, but they are simple. Life complicates things. Rivalries, old wounds from battles long ago, jealousy—there are lots of things that cloud our judgment.

Jesus had a great way of crafting parables that exposed how people had gotten balled up in those complications. Parables that blew away the fog and exposed the simple answer. The simple answer is to drive po-litely everywhere, especially on Johnston Street. If we see a Samaritan trying to merge into traffic, let's ease off and let him in.

And He said, "A man had two sons. The younger of them said to his father, 'Father, give me the share of the estate that falls to me.' So he divided his wealth between them. And not many days later, the younger son gathered everything together and went on a journey into a distant country, and there he squandered his estate with loose living. Now when he had spent everything, a severe famine occurred in that country, and he began to be impoverished. So he went and hired himself out to one of the citizens of that country, and he sent him into his fields to feed swine. And he would have gladly filled his stomach with the pods that the swine were eating, and no one was giving anything to him.

"But when he came to his senses, he said, 'How many of my father's hired men have more than enough bread, but I am dying here with hunger! I will get up and go to my father, and will say to him, "Father, I have sinned against heaven, and in your sight; I am no longer worthy to be called your son; make me as one of your hired men."' So he got up and came to his father. But while he was still a long way off, his father saw him and felt compassion for him, and ran and embraced him and kissed him. And the son said to him, 'Father, I have sinned against heaven and in your sight; I am no longer worthy to be called your son.' But the father said to his slaves, 'Quickly bring out the best robe and put it on him, and put a ring on his hand and sandals on his feet; and bring the fattened calf, kill it, and let us eat and celebrate; for this son of mine was dead and has come to life again; he was lost and has been found.' And they began to celebrate.

"Now his older son was in the field, and when he came and approached the house, he heard music and dancing. And he summoned one of the servants and began inquiring what these things could be. And

he said to him, 'Your brother has come, and your father has killed the fattened calf because he has received him back safe and sound.' But he became angry and was not willing to go in; and his father came out and began pleading with him. But he answered and said to his father, 'Look! For so many years I have been serving you and I have never neglected a command of yours; and yet you have never given me a young goat, so that I might celebrate with my friends; but when this son of yours came, who has devoured your wealth with prostitutes, you killed the fattened calf for him.' And he said to him, 'Son, you have always been with me, and all that is mine is yours. But we had to celebrate and rejoice, for this brother of yours was dead and has begun to live, and was lost and has been found.'"

—Luke 15:11–32 (English Standard Version)

Matt Deggs is the head coach of the UL Lafayette baseball team. As of this writing, he had led the Cajuns to the NCAA tournament in 2022 and 2023, after working through the challenges the COVID-19 pandemic presented college athletics the previous two years.

He is a talented coach, always has been. His career took off when he was an assistant coach for Division I schools, and it was a meteoric rise that projected success for the duration of his career.

And then he got sidetracked.

Substance abuse consumed him for a period of time and nearly ended his coaching career permanently. Perform an online search of "Matt Deggs tribulations" if you want to hear what he worked through. Better yet, read his book entitled *15 to 28*.

He is a powerful speaker and is very open about his journey. He is equally powerful in conveying his gratitude to Tony Robichaux, who brought him on as an assistant coach when the profession had given up on Matt Deggs.

Repentance is a key component of Christianity. Virtually every Christian service at some point, often at the beginning of the service, calls upon those in attendance to acknowledge that they have fallen short of the glory of God. Repentance by the older son is at the heart of the parable of the prodigal son.

On the other side of this parable, some of us will have the opportunity to welcome back a prodigal son in the same manner as the father in today's scripture. Not many, however.

Most all of us will have to live out this scripture in small acts. The way we respond when our spouse apologizes for something done, the way we react when a motorist slides into traffic ahead of us but does not slow us down, the way we treat a waiter who is trying to help us enjoy our meal.

All these small daily interactions are opportunities either to focus inward and be resentful or to be joyous for the actions of another person. We get to decide. Every day.

DAY 21

The Jews there were amazed and asked, "How did this man get such learning without having been taught?"

—John 7:15 (New International Version)

The Hilliard Art Museum is a beautiful architectural structure that was the result of a gift by Paul Hilliard and his late wife, Lulu. Paul Hilliard is one of the self-made entrepreneurs talked about on day 15.

The Lafayette Science Museum was the product of a community effort to build a quality museum in Lafayette. That effort began in the 1970s, and the original structure was across from Girard Park, behind the Heymann Performing Arts Center. It was called the Lafayette Planetarium and was noted for its star shows. Later the museum was moved to its current location in downtown Lafayette.

The Children's Museum of Acadiana was another product of the community, which resolved in the 1990s to stand up a children's museum in Lafayette. It sits in downtown Lafayette, across the street from the science museum. These are all great facilities that provide the opportunity to learn and grow outside a formal classroom setting.

There is a tendency to think that the "right" school is the only path to intellectual achievement, to discernment, to understanding.

Perhaps Jesus best demonstrates the flaw in that thinking. The Pharisees were the intellectuals of that time. Yet they could not get their minds wrapped around the fact that people were flocking to some carpenter's kid from a backwater town named Nazareth. It really blew their minds. Jesus ended up spending a lot of time explaining things to the Pharisees. The Pharisees' reaction was not to reflect on what corrections or changes they needed to make. Instead, it was to wonder "Where does He get this from?"

Intellectual curiosity, a desire to improve, a motivation to acquire a deeper understanding of a topic, a yearning to have a deeper appreciation of a work of art—these really are universal desires. We strive to be better today than we were yesterday and be better tomorrow than we are today. Sometimes a formal, traditional education path is the best way to channel that energy in the right direction. However, there are many people who became wildly successful after (because?) they left the formal, traditional education path and charted a new course.

Learning is a habit. Intellectual curiosity is a habit. Persistence is a habit. Exercise is a habit. What's more, these are habits everyone can adopt. Adopting the right habits is vitally important.

Here's another thought to ruminate on. Maybe, just maybe, it is a good idea to make reading the Bible a habit too. We can carve out time every day. The Bible is too big, we say. Well, let's take it one chapter at a time, one book at a time. Habitually.

DAY 22

Congratulations. You have reached day twenty-two of this thirty-day devotional.

Father Chester Arceneaux once delivered a wonderful homily about habits. He pointed out that a habit is just something you do twenty-one days in a row.

If you are here on day twenty-two, you are in the habit of reading a daily devotional. You are also nearing the end of this particular devotional.

Now is the time to plan for your next devotional to keep your reading going (now that you are in the habit).

Scan the QR code below to access a list of options.

Choose one that interests you and order it online, or go out and find your next devotional at a bookstore near you. Just keep up your Bible-reading habit.

Today's message is on the following page. Hope it is a thoughtful message that helps us build on the daily habit of reading the Bible.

And I tell you that you are Peter, and on this rock I will build my church, and the gates of Hades will not overcome it.

—Matt. 16:18 (New International Version)

Southwestern Louisiana Industrial Institute (SLII) was created through state legislation in 1898. Robert Martin of St. Martin Parish introduced what would become Act 162.

By 1920, the school changed to a four-year course culminating with a bachelor of arts degree, and the next year the school was renamed the Southwestern Louisiana Institute of Liberal and Technical Learning, or SLI. The mascot was a bulldog.

By 1960, the school was renamed the University of Southwestern Louisiana (USL). The school was again renamed in 1999, becoming the University of Louisiana at Lafayette (UL Lafayette). Somewhere in between those two changes, the school sports teams became known as the Ragin' Cajuns.

An interesting note as a follow-up to day 4's discussion of churches in the area involves the Our Lady of Wisdom Church and Catholic Student Center. It sits on the campus of UL Lafayette and was the first in Louisiana to be built on state land.

UL Lafayette now has the largest enrollment within the nine-campus University of Louisiana system and the second-largest enrollment in Louisiana. It has also become a top-tier research university, designated among doctoral universities as having "very high research activity."

Simon underwent a name change to Peter, and along with it Jesus declared that Peter was the rock upon which the church was to be built.

Our Lady of Wisdom Church

Institutions can and often do grow and improve in ways not imagined by the founders of the organization.

People do too. They can grow and improve to accomplish things that no one thought possible. Simon was a fisherman; no one thought of him as the rock that the church was to be built upon. Saul of Tarsus was a terror, but he was changed into an instrument of good works and the author of many of the books of the New Testament.

Jesus changed many lives during His time on this earth. His message, His teachings, and His example literally changed the entire world and still change lives today. His message was here yesterday, is here today, and will be here tomorrow. We just have to read it.

DAY 23

So they set out from the mountain of the LORD and traveled for three
days. The ark of the covenant of the LORD went before them during
those three days to find them a place to rest.

— Num. 10:33 (New International Version)

Bendel Gardens is a subdivision in Lafayette bordered by the Vermilion River, Pinhook Road, Bendel Road, and College Drive. It is a subdivision of less than 200 homes, an established footprint (the bordering roads prevent expansion), mature oak trees, and a mix of stately and recently renovated homes.

Henri Bendel was born in what was then called Vermilionville in 1868. He opened millinery shops in Lafayette and Houma ("millinery" means the manufacturing and craft of making hats and headwear, by the way). In 1895, he moved to New York City and opened a women's department store that catered to upper-class women and bore his name, Henri Bendel, Inc. Cole Porter's tune "You're the Top" mentions a Bendel bonnet in the lyrics. The Goldring/Woldenberg Institute of Southern Jewish Life has a more thorough biography of Henri Bendel on its website if you are interested in his journey from Vermilionville to New York.

He also acquired 180 acres of land along the Vermilion River, a property called the Walnut Grove Plantation, where he built a home that he reportedly named Camellia Lodge. Despite his success in New York City, he never forgot his family in Lafayette, making occasional trips back home until his death in 1936.

The land he purchased was subdivided in the 1950s to create the Bendel Gardens subdivision.

It is a long way from Lafayette to New York, and not the easiest of trips. It was an even tougher trip in the early twentieth century. Now imagine walking from town to town. No motorized vehicles, no inter-states, no directional signs, no rest stops, not even a Buc-ee's.

One takeaway from Numbers 10 is that God desires to be with His people. That is why the ark of the covenant existed and why they carried it everywhere.

This scripture also reminds us how the Israelites traveled great distances in the Old Testament. The disciples walked great distances spreading Jesus's message in the New Testament. These were arduous journeys guided by faith, and in the end they were worth the effort.

Our journeys now are vastly different from those of the Israelites and the disciples. The main challenge then was finding shelter along the route from city to city. Our challenge is to stay within the speed limit, avoid drunk drivers, find a safe hotel, and not get stuck on Interstate 10 between Lafayette and Baton Rouge. Very different challenges, but challenges nonetheless.

Getting from point A to point B was a challenge then. While it is very, very different, it is a challenge now. Studying the Bible and trying to practice a little Christianity can be a challenge as well. It requires persistence, focus, and dedication, but it is worth it.

DAY 24

We proclaim to you what we have seen and heard, so that you also may have fellowship with us. And our fellowship is with the Father and with his Son, Jesus Christ. We write this to make our joy complete.

—1 John 1:3–7 (New International Version)

They devoted themselves to the apostles' teaching and to fellowship, to the breaking of bread and to prayer.

—Acts 2:42 (New International Version)

The Greater Southwest Mardi Gras Association coordinates Mardi Gras in Lafayette.

Mardi Gras krewes are individual groups of people that band together to enjoy Mardi Gras. There are about fifty krewes in Lafayette, most all of which have a ball and designate royalty to honor each year. Some are very old krewes, some are children's krewes, and some are newly formed.

About ten of the krewes have floats that participate in the parades that roll through the city.

The point is that there is a krewe for everyone if someone is interested in participating in a Mardi Gras krewe and willing to make a financial commitment. If not, you get to enjoy the parades for free.

We were meant to be in a community to share successes, to support each other through adversity, to encourage one another, and to enjoy one another's company. Hebrews 10:24–25 encourages us to explore how we can spur one another toward love and good deeds and encourage one another to continue the habit of meeting together.

Book clubs, hobby-focused clubs, service clubs, and even exercise groups are all—on some level—social organizations. Reunions are just a way to revisit a community from an earlier time.

Mardi Gras krewes are just social organizations centered on Mardi Gras (so they get to throw beads). However, no matter the social organization's focus, it is a community. We are social beings.

Church congregations are communities as well. Part of what a church congregation does is to foster social interaction. That is what prayer groups are for. That is what small groups are for. That is what Sunday school is for. That is what congregations facilitate. Congregations gather to worship as a community, to have fellowship, to sing, and to celebrate.

However, church congregations are more than social communities. They are communities centered on the Bible and focused on living into and spreading Jesus's message. Worth embracing, and worth joining, even if you don't get to throw beads...

DAY 25

Do you not know that your body is a temple of the Holy Spirit within you, whom you have from God, and that you are not your own?

—1 Cor. 6:19 (New American Bible)

Red's is both an institution and a continually improving fitness facility. It was started by Red Lerille, a former Mr. America, in 1963. It has operated at its current location since 1965. It is an impressive physical plant, with an array of options that remove any excuse for not working out. Bring friends in from a town with a population of a million or more, let them walk around Red's, and listen to their amazement.

Red is another of the entrepreneurs referenced on an earlier devotional page. He combined his passion for fitness with sound business decisions and built a world-class facility. What's more, he has transferred management of that facility to the next generation. The second generation has built on that foundation and continues to develop and improve the facility.

It is easy now to have lots of things done for us. Want a pizza? Want our groceries selected and packaged up? Want to get something shipped to our house? Those things that used to draw on our energy are now effortless—just a few clicks away on the mobile device we carry with us.

What do we do with that "extra" time technology and customer service have created? Self-indulgence is certainly an option. While the tasks of everyday life have been made easier, the options for self-indulgence are more plentiful than ever.

If only there were guidance…and yet there is. There are multiple verses on the importance of discipline in the New Testament.

The body is the temple of the Lord. This is a simple biblical anchor. Exercise, eat healthy, go outdoors, breathe fresh air. Simple things. Wellness really isn't that complicated.

The first point is that some people fall in love with their temple a bit too much and start worshipping it instead of the Lord. Let's not lose sight of things. We worship in a temple; we don't worship the temple.

The second point is that stewardship means caring for the things in our possession. That includes the body that God blessed us with, which means everyone should engage in "temple maintenance."

DAY 26

They came to him and said, "Teacher, we know that you are a man of integrity. You aren't swayed by others, because you pay no attention to who they are; but you teach the way of God in accordance with the truth. Is it right to pay the imperial tax to Caesar or not? Should we pay or shouldn't we?"

But Jesus knew their hypocrisy. "Why are you trying to trap me?" he asked. "Bring me a denarius and let me look at it." They brought the coin, and he asked them, "Whose image is this? And whose inscription?" "Caesar's," they replied. Then Jesus said to them, "Give back to Caesar what is Caesar's and to God what is God's."

—Mark 12:14–17 (New International Version)

Lafayette is one of about fifty local governments in the country where the city and the parish (county) are consolidated. This arrangement has helped minimize the fighting between those in the city and those outside the incorporated area. It makes the Mayor-President more attuned to the entirety of the area, rather than one specific geographic subset of the area.

The Lafayette metropolitan area (which includes the surrounding parishes) just eclipsed Shreveport-Bossier as the third largest area in the state. Sure must be doing something right.

But the Lafayette City-Parish Consolidated Government—like all civilian governments—has its limits. That is by design. While it does have a sphere of authority, it is not all-powerful.

Jesus did not come to balance Caesar's budget. He did not come to rule the Roman Empire (although he could have). He declined in this scripture to get into parochial discussions about who was "in charge." It is all too easy to get lost in the weeds or go down a rabbit hole in those types of debates.

We all worship something. That is what thinking human beings do. It may be Prada shoes; it may be a performing artist; it may be an athlete or a designer. Some people worship government and put those "in charge" on a high pedestal. We will worship something. There is something that our minds drift off to during a lull in the workday, something that is the focus of our energy, and something that we center our plans on. We will worship something.

Shoes fall into and out of fashion (and they wear out); performing artists get eclipsed by the latest new thing; players retire. One way or another, a public official's term will end.

If we are going to worship something, think of it this way: why not worship a presence that came two thousand years ago, was crucified, died and was buried, rose from the dead, and ascended into heaven to show us how much He cares for us? His message and sacrifice inspired disciples, who inspired thousands, who inspired millions. His teachings, message, and sacrifice continue to inspire and guide people today.

Jesus came to explain and to demonstrate the way to approach life's challenges, and He died on a cross to show us how much God wants us to follow that way.

DAY 27

So he came again to Cana in Galilee, where he had made the water wine.

—John 4:46 (English Standard Version)

La Fonda is an institution in Lafayette. A Tex-Mex restaurant with sturdy frozen drinks, it has stood in the same location since 1957.

The walls are adorned with headshot portraits of its frequent visitors who are prominent in the community. If you have not had the pleasure of going there, put "La Fonda 1957 history" in your search engine to see pictures of the interior. The menu remains straightforward and essentially unchanged.

It is a landmark for seemingly every Lafayette resident ("Is that street before or after La Fonda?" "Is that store on the LaFonda side or the other side of the road?").

The name is, at this point, part of the lexicon of Lafayette. It is instantly recognizable, invariably evokes a positive memory or response, and is associated with the town.

The phrase "turning water into wine" is part of the lexicon too. Pretty much everyone understands the notion being conveyed and that it is from the Bible.

The verse above is part of the scripture describing the miracle at the wedding in Cana.

The first point to make is that there are people in our society that struggle with alcoholism. The miracle at the wedding in Cana demonstrates His sovereignty; it is not the story of an open bar at a wedding reception. In an earlier devotional, we discussed the call to discipline that recurs throughout the New Testament.

The second point is to emphasize that the Bible is foundational to our civilization. It has been studied, read, and analyzed for over two thousand years. Its phrases, exhortations, wisdom, teachings, and guidance are interwoven into our society.

Funny thing—the more we read the Bible, the more we start to identify phrases, sayings, and references that are part of our lexicon. There are a lot of these that have permeated the culture over the centuries, as they should have.

It has been said that the Bible is a sixty-six-book love story, and who doesn't appreciate reading a good love story? Along the way do not be surprised if you find yourself saying "So that's where that phrase comes from."

DAY 28

"Let us build up these towns," he said to Judah, *"and put walls around them, with towers, gates and bars. The land is still ours, because we have sought the Lord our God; we sought him and he has given us rest on every side." So they built and prospered.*

—2 Chron. 14:7 (New International Version)

Maurice Heymann is another of the entrepreneurs who came to the area, built prosperity for himself, and enriched the community with his financial support. He was born in New Orleans in 1885, but Lafayette was a perfect fit for him because his mother was French. The Goldring/Woldenberg Institute of Southern Jewish Life has a more thorough biography of Maurice Heyman on its website if you are interested in his career that began as a New Orleanian with a sixth-grade education working as a butcher boy selling meat on the Pontchartrain Railroad, and ended with him being a highly successful businessman in Lafayette. Once here he recognized a potential market among the local Native American community, Heymann was able to peddle his wares successfully enough to purchase his first store in Lafayette in 1916. In 1937 he opened a "food center" in his Lafayette department store, which became the city's first supermarket.

His contributions to Lafayette's Mardi Gras are outlined in another devotional. In addition to his contribution to facilitate Lafayette General, as described below, he also made a significant contribution toward the construction of Our Lady of Lourdes

Hospital, as discussed in the day 17 devotional. Maurice Heymann was the winner of Lafayette's first Civic Cup Award for his community involvement.

Maurice Heymann's most lasting impact on Lafayette was his development of the Heymann Oil Center in 1952, which was built to capitalize on Texas- and Lake Charles–area oil companies relocating their production to the Gulf Coast. The "Hub City" was close to the Gulf and was large enough for conducting business, so oil companies flocked to Lafayette. The arrangement was that no building would be constructed in the Oil Center unless there was a lease in place covering the cost of construction.

The Oil Center also includes the Petroleum Club. The story goes that a group of oil executives approached Heymann about constructing a "club room." He embraced the idea and agreed to contribute the land if the oil executives constructed the building. The Petroleum Club was officially opened April 12, 1953. Although it was once a private dining space for oil executives, it has been open to the public since 1986.

Maurice Heymann continued to invest in the area adjoining the Oil Center. The Heymann Performing Arts Center opened in 1960, and Lafayette General Hospital relocated there five years later. Both were built on property he owned. Today, the Oil Center remains a close-knit community of offices, restaurants, and shops.

Stewardship means caring for the things with which we are entrusted. Sometimes that means preserving, caring for, and maintaining things: our family's photos, the neighbor's dog, our grandmother's wedding ring.

However, sometimes it means developing and improving those things with which we are entrusted. Taking the assets we have at our disposal, applying our time and talents, and producing more assets: a useful chair, a beautiful space, greater wealth, or a higher standard of living.

The parable of the bags of gold found in Matthew 25 speaks to this. The servant who invested and grew the assets he was entrusted with was celebrated. The servant who hoarded the assets he was entrusted with was scorned. We are called to use the assets we are blessed with to improve, to grow, and to better our own lives and the lives of those around us.

DAY 29

A large crowd of his disciples was there and a great number of people from all over Judea, from Jerusalem, and from the coastal region around Tyre and Sidon, who had come to hear him and to be healed of their diseases. Those troubled by impure spirits were cured, and the people all tried to touch him, because power was coming from him and healing them all.

—Luke 6:17–19 (New International Version)

The UL Lafayette Athletic Department website (ragincajuns.com) has a more detailed history of Cajun Field, which has served as the home of Ragin' Cajuns football since September 1971. The stadium has undergone changes twice in its history to increase capacity. The first was in 1992 to increase the capacity to 31,000. The second was to update the seating in the south end zone prior to the 2014 season and expand the capacity to 41,426.

Perhaps the greatest moment for football at Cajun Field came during the 1996 season when the Ragin' Cajuns opened their twenty-sixth season in the facility with the biggest upset in school history, a 29–22 victory over number twenty-five Texas A&M in front of a then-record crowd of 38,783. A Sun Belt Conference record 32,823 attended the North Texas game on October 15, 2011. The all-time record for attendance was set on September 5, 2009, when the Ragin' Cajuns defeated Southern University 42–19. The Ragin' Cajuns are 139–112–2 all time at the stadium through the 2022 season.

Cajun Field, recently renamed Our Lady of Lourdes Stadium

UL Lafayette just unveiled plans to renovate the stadium, and those renovations are scheduled to be completed by the start of the 2025 season. As part of the project, the stadium has been renamed Our Lady of Lourdes Stadium.

During the tenure of Dr. Ray Authement, there were no Saturday-afternoon football games scheduled. He believed such activities would take away from shopping activities. (This viewpoint also fostered a robust tailgating experience for Ragin' Cajun home football games.)

There were no stadiums in the Middle East at the time of Jesus's ministry. No bleachers providing elevated seating, no suites, no public-address systems to broadcast His message.

We get impressed by large, imposing structures like football stadiums. We get enamored with the trappings of those facilities. The scoreboard with real-time statistics, the video that allows you to see the last play again, the music blasted out between breaks in the action, concessions that are a short walk away, the chairback seats (or better yet, the suites in the press box)—all these trappings have become integral to the game-day experience.

Jesus simply spoke to crowds, and the crowds grew during the course of His ministry. The words He spoke helped His followers fully grasp his message. Sometimes He drew on history; sometimes He used parables; sometimes He responded to queries. He articulated how His followers should act and even gave us a prayer. His words were delivered in a simple, uncomplicated way, but the message was powerful. His message, His teachings, His sacrifice—they are worth experiencing through reading scripture. His words are worth reading. Every day.

Therefore go and make disciples of all nations, baptizing them in the name of the Father and of the Son and of the Holy Spirit.

— Matt. 28:19 (New International Version)

The Lafayette Convention and Visitors Commission (LCVC) is charged with promoting the city and parish of Lafayette for purposes of conventions and tourism, and to encourage the development of tourist attractions in the Lafayette area.

If you are ever looking for something to do, or if you are trying to schedule something and want to know what may create a conflict, the LCVC website is a good place to start.

The mission of LCVC is, so to speak, to spread the gospel of Lafayette. Of course all of us are ambassadors for Lafayette on some level. When we travel, our interactions with others reflect on us and also our area. You may be the only Lafayette resident that person ever meets.

Similarly, you may be the first Lafayette resident a visitor to our area meets. As we know, first impressions matter.

Today's scripture is a simple declaration, but it leads us to a much, much larger discussion of what the church is challenged to do in twenty-first-century America. At the outset of this devotional, we declared that each day's devotional was designed so that the reader had to carve out a small amount of time to get through it. We will hold true to that commitment, but know that a full discussion and analysis of the challenge of this scripture would take far more than two or three pages.

Part of what we are called to do is to share the good news and show why Jesus's message is the right way to approach things. There is no shortage of folks who want to make things complicated. Jesus spent a fair amount of time explaining things simply.

Leading by example is another way to share the faith. Jesus showed people what the message looked like in action. WWJD (What Would Jesus Do?) is a way to get people to try to utilize Jesus's actions, His example, when searching for how to react to a situation. Our actions can influence others to realize that what Jesus would do is the right way to approach things.

First Baptist Church

There are many ways to win people over. Humor. Success. Achievement. Empathy. Camaraderie. Commonality. Thankfulness. Intelligence. Kindness. Courtesy. Attentiveness. Politeness. Honesty. Forthrightness. Efficiency. Effectiveness. Courage. Steadfastness.

So many tools in the toolbox. Which one is right? Well, that turns on the situation and the person we are interacting with. Each one of us is an ambassador for our city and our faith.

The point here is this: part of what we are called to do is to make disciples of Christ. The specific strategy and technique we utilize in a given situation is something we can debate. That we are called to do it is not.

LAGNIAPPE

We picked up one excellent word—a word worth traveling to New Orleans to get; a nice limber, expressive, hand word—"lagniappe." They pronounce it lanny-yap... The custom originated in the Spanish quarter of the city.

—Mark Twain describing the word "lagniappe" in his book Life on the Mississippi, published in 1883

"Lagniappe" in New Orleans originally meant a present given to customers who purchase groceries or other items at retail stores, especially to children. Children were said in the old days of New Orleans not only to look forward to their lagniappes but also to ask for them. Grocery stores, especially, competed for business by trying to put together the best lagniappes, whether these were baked treats or other sweets or fruits. The tradition in New Orleans came to mean any small gift given to a customer at the time of purchase.

The notion of lagniappe spread to Lafayette long, long ago. It is often described in Lafayette as "a little something extra." It could be a gift, or it might be an extra helping of food.

In this case, the lagniappe takes the form of a few extra days of devotionals to give the reader time to make sure the next devotional has been secured. Hope this devotional lagniappe is enriching and the next devotional is secured soon.

DAY 31

After this I looked, and there before me was a great multitude that no one could count, from every nation, tribe, people and language, standing before the throne and before the Lamb. They were wearing white robes and were holding palm branches in their hands.

—Rev. 7:9 (New International Version)

The population statistics for Lafayette were listed earlier in the devotional, and it should be noted there is no mention of a Lebanese demographic in the official statistics. Some may find it odd that in Lafayette—the area occupied by the Attakapas Indians, settled by Acadians, and populated by the English—there would be a strong Lebanese community. But there is.

Street names, businesses, and athletic programs project the strong presence of the Lebanese community in Lafayette. Abdalla, Ackal, Ashy, Boustany, Joseph, Haik, Mahfouz, Mahtook, Saloom—these are all prominent families in the area. It is always perilous to generalize about a demographic; as we pointed out in an earlier devotional, every individual is blessed with special and unique talents and gifts. However, even a casual observer in Lafayette would note that it is a deeply Catholic community.

Here's a tip: if you are ever invited to a dinner party thrown by a Lebanese family, go! You will likely have a great mix of family, faith, food, drink, and wonderful stories.

We don't immediately think of a family grape leaf-rolling party when we think of Lafayette (again, if you are ever invited to one, go!), but that happens here.

We inherently know the value of community. Unfortunately, a lot of the time, technology pushes us away from interaction with others. Community, family, and friends help us get through the valleys of life and help us celebrate the high points of the journey. Those gatherings of family…they are an opportunity for different generations to interact. A transfer of information from one generation to the next, the passing down of the wisdom of the ages.

The Bible gives us guidance and also contains the wisdom of the ages. Proverbs is properly named; it is loaded with proverbs. The ten commandments are located in two places in the Old Testament. The point being that the Bible contains a wealth of guidance on the challenges we face. We just need to read it.

DAY 32

After this, Jesus traveled about from one town and village to another, proclaiming the good news of the kingdom of God. The Twelve were with him…

—Luke 8:1 (New International Version)

There are a number of walking areas in Lafayette. Girard Park, with its walking path running through the park, and Moncus Park, with its loop around the exterior of the park, are two that come to mind.

Virtually every park operated by the Lafayette City-Parish Consolidated Government has a walking path of some type integrated into it. There are also little hidden gems like the path off Lake Farm Road or the path around Our Lady of Lourdes Hospital. Paths like that are located all across the area. There are also lots of neighborhoods where walking down the street is both expected and accommodated.

(There are more than a half dozen good golf courses too. Golflink. com gives a good rundown of the courses in the area. However, as Mark Twain once said, "Golf is a good walk spoiled.")

Walking was fairly integral to the spreading of Jesus's message. Jesus walked from town to town. So did His disciples as they fanned out across the region to spread the good news. Funny thing—while Jesus walked a lot, He is never described as walking in a hurry.

Walking is one of those activities that is so simple yet so good for us. There are simple answers: spend less than our take-home pay and save the rest, exercise, enjoy the outdoors, spend time talking with friends.

Life seems complex, but maybe it isn't. There have always been challenges. One hundred years ago, the challenges were to find food, good working conditions, and information. Today we are swamped with information and choices. The challenges are control, discretion, and discernment.

How do we deal with information overload? Download. Clear your head with a good walk (bring your golf clubs along if you are on the course). Process the information you have been deluged with. Walking helps us to slow down life and makes it easier to enjoy the company of others. Walking helped produce great things in Jesus's time. So did His message. The same is still true today for both.

DAY 33

You are the light of the world. A town built on a hill cannot be hidden.

—Matt. 5:14 (New International Version)

At sixty feet above sea level, Orlando Mountain has a name and has been declared the highest point in Lafayette, Louisiana.

It is the big hill in Moncus Park that overlooks the hundred-acre green space and has nice views of Lafayette. That big hill has officially been named Orlando Mountain because of the generosity of Steve and Lisa Orlando. In a way it is an artificial hill, but it is sixty feet above sea level.

Matthew 5 is a treasure, chock full of wisdom, thoughts, and guidance. The image of the city on a hill, for example, inspired Americans in the nineteenth and twentieth centuries. Ronald Reagan often quoted it. As a result there are lots of scholarly articles dissecting the use of this scripture.

If we stand on Orlando Mountain, someone will see us. We could stand on Orlando Mountain and create chaos or behave badly, but why would we want to do that? Why would we squander that opportunity and further diminish things? If you are going to stand on a mountaintop, be a source of inspiration, of pride. Be a positive example.

Our actions influence those around us. We can be a positive influence or a negative influence, but we will be an influence on some level. What will we use this influence for? To convince someone not to try, to help persuade the person that the task is too hard, that not striving to improve is the better course? That is not the message Jesus brought us.

He spoke of the value of every human being, the potential that exists in each one of us.

There is a simple truth to this verse. A city on a hill cannot be hidden. If that is the case, better to make it look good, because its flaws are easily seen. Be an example; be a good example. One that is worthy of emulation, and one that contributes to the upward march of humanity.

Paul and Timothy's letter to Philippi was likely written from prison. Paul established the church there, and the letter was written to encourage that community. It is worth a full reading and analysis, but a couple of points present themselves. First, it is a letter. We earlier talked about the power of a letter.

Second, we have tried to convey what a wonderful resource the Bible is. What better way to underscore that point than to conclude this devotional by quoting scripture?

Paul and Timothy succinctly exhort the community in the final portion of this letter. The words are as relevant now as they were more than two thousand years ago, and what they wrote then applies to us today:

Do not be anxious about anything, but in every situation, by prayer and petition, with thanksgiving, present your requests to God. And the peace of God, which transcends all understanding, will guard your hearts and your minds in Christ Jesus.

Finally, brothers and sisters, whatever is true, whatever is noble, whatever is right, whatever is pure, whatever is lovely, whatever is admirable—if anything is excellent or praiseworthy—think about such things. Whatever you have learned or received or heard from me, or seen in me—put it into practice. And the God of peace will be with you. (Philippians 4:6–9 [New International Version])

ACKNOWLEDGMENTS

It is truly rewarding to have the opportunity to develop this devotional. However, I had lots of help, input, and guidance in this project.

Marilyn Lee was an accomplished photographer long before I started developing this devotional. She was gracious in allowing me to include her work and generous with her time in suggesting (and taking) photos that worked with the particular day of the devotional. Her contact info is on the book cover (little_dog_creative on Instagram). What was included in this devotional is the tip of the iceberg. If you like her work, there is plenty more to enjoy.

Dr. Bryan Sibley has been a good friend and trusted advisor for many, many years. In the midst of becoming a grandfather (again), he found time to review drafts of the devotional and provide edits and suggestions. He is an author (look for his book *God First*), and so his insight and guidance were invaluable.

Marc Mouton, who wrote the foreword to the devotional, is a walking encyclopedia of Lafayette history. He provided relevant nuggets of Lafayette history that I likely could never have chased down. He double-checked the history to help confirm its accuracy. This is a devotional, not a history book. If there are mistakes, they are mine. However, his time and energy made it a much richer and more accurate recitation of Lafayette's history.

Several people were kind enough to read through the drafts and give me feedback and suggestions. Members of my nuclear family, including Mary Morgan Stipe, Rowe Stipe, and Jeigh Stipe, were tremendously helpful. Mary Morgan Stipe left a flurry of Post-its with observations. Rowe and I had several lengthy conversations about the points raised and made and the content of each day's devotional. Jeigh Stipe provided support and thoughts throughout the entire process.

My sister, Marie Stipe, read the first draft and gave me great feedback about the devotional. Father Wayne Duet has been giving me guidance for decades (literally), and that guidance is embedded in the pages of this devotional. Rev. Scott Bullock was kind enough to read through the devotional, and he gave me some great input.

Chris Hockaday lives in Conway, Arkansas, but lived in Lafayette for a period of time. That perspective was extremely valuable in helping me articulate some of the points and history that are included.

Sonny Chastain, who was also in the midst of becoming a grandfather (again), spent a great deal of time analyzing and critiquing the drafts. His insight greatly enhanced the quality of this devotional.

Thanks to Palmetto Publishing for the guidance, support, and experienced advice. The team members were generous with their time and suggestions, and they deserve a great deal of credit for the end product.

Milton Keynes UK
Ingram Content Group UK Ltd.
UKHW022032111223
434204UK00006B/180